MINISTRY DEVELOPING MANUAL

AL MENEFEE

WestBow
PRESS
A DIVISION OF THOMAS NELSON

WestBow Press books may be ordered through booksellers or by contacting:

WestBow Press
A Division of Thomas Nelson
1663 Liberty Drive
Bloomington, IN 47403
www.westbowpress.com
1-(866) 928-1240

ISBN: 978-1-4497-3156-4 (sc)
ISBN: 978-1-4497-3157-1 (e)

Library of Congress Control Number: 2011960684

Printed in the United States of America

WestBow Press rev. date: 12/08/2011

INTRODUCTION

After multiple meetings with the men's ministry, discussing topics on spiritual development, I have developed an order of helpful articles and instruments that I believe will help accomplish that goal.

I believe that a man must first understand and accept his spiritual purpose before he can receive the knowledge of his spiritual gift(s). The importance of knowing the spiritual gift(s) is as vital as knowing the family genealogy, chains without broken links, the alphabet. Gifts make everything work in order to fulfill God's purpose. Our world is an example of how without order, chaos, murder, deceit, to name a few, exist. With gifts operating as God intended, love would be the rock upon which all foundations would be built. For gifts were not meant just for you, but as a universal link to others for God's glory and purpose to be revealed.

Let this manual be a starting point for development of avenues of approach in developing knowledge of spiritual gifts. God reveals his missions to whomever he desireth. When we elevate ourselves among men, the effect is short lived. God's chosen are not earthly seekers, but believers of the message. In Luke 1:50; "The weak fear God and praise Him." Stay weak and fear God, I pray for each and everyone.

Al Menefee

WHAT IT MEANS TO SERVE

There are numerous ways to define the word "serve" making it very fluid or active. It can be applied by groups or individually.

As a servant of Christ, I'm actively applying the term both ways. I learned at an early age the group indoctrination to Christianity by attending church. It was through this group training I learned the basics for my Christian development and walk with Christ. It seemed fair to me because at school, I was expected to learn and accept the academic courses that would lead to my success in this life. I was expected to complete the grammar and high school curriculum, then college, believing that a good job and life for me would be my reward. So, my obedience to parental guidance and professional instructions commenced.

Along the way, in my development, I discovered that my Christian development had a personal, individual component different from my academic development. I saw broken lives of men and women who didn't develop a strong relationship with God. I also saw men and women who were successful that had no relationship with God. I was confused and troubled. But when I applied my personal relationship with the God I serve, He revealed himself to me individually. My prayers were answered directly and without alternatives or second guesses. The greatest answer to my prayers was that this life is not eternal; therefore, I should learn what it takes to achieve eternal life.

My best years were spent in pursuit of earthly possessions. Although taught different, I allowed my Christian development to be overtaken by my quest at academic excellence which would lead to "the good life." I became a servant of things and others. The disappointments and losses were constant yet I failed to connect them with my exclusion of Christ whom I knew. Yes, I was a servant, but not of Christ.

My life became clear when I returned to where I stopped developing spirituality. It was as though I'd never left because of the forgiving nature of the God I serve. He put me back on my path and renewed my ability to hear and see his will. I only had to become a willing vessel that he could use. By willing, I mean to allow my flesh to decrease in order for his spirit to increase. I no longer wanted my mind, but His. My whole body had to be sacrificed in order for Him to act through me. I prayed that he be revealed in me so others could see only him not me. This was just one of many prayers I prayed in order to confirm His existence. My intent has never been to provoke or test God. By praying to be worthy as one of His vessels, He has confirmed through His usage of me, His existence. I have moved from a "spiritual hopeful" to a "spiritual servant." I no longer hope He hears my prayers or that He will use me. He manifests himself in me daily even though I yet fall short of his glory daily. My heart He knows, and that I work to learn of Him and his desire for me continues His mercy.

This mission, then, is a minor remnant of the whole quilt God is sewing. When we see the many pieces of a quilt sewn together, we see a finished cohesive product; every piece complimenting the other in order to achieve the same goal. Many of us have God's remnants tucked away in some obscure place where it can't be sewn into God's quilt. At a recent bible study, I learned of the "napkin," from the resurrection of Christ that was left in the tomb. It is said to have been left in such a manner that infers a human form could not remove itself from it without leaving it disheveled or disturbed. Some say it represented a cultural tradition whereby if the napkin was left undisturbed it indicated to the servants the master was not finished and would be back. If the napkin was disturbed and left, it meant the master was finished.

I see both positions of the napkin as it pertains to this my first mission for Christ. He left the napkin undisturbed to signify this human life for him was over. That it was finished. It also indicates to me that as our spiritual Father and Savior, he would be coming back again.

I fear God but love his mercy because mercy endureth forever. His mercy restores my soul when earthly troubles seem insurmountable. My life's journey has taught me that as a sheep of God I have his protection and victory over any adversity. When I doubt I have learned to find a quiet place and wait for his directions, He continuously provides me with alternatives for this life crisis because I lean only on Him. In the Shepherd's Prayer, " . . . He leadeth me in the path of righteousness for his name sake . . ." the meaning is clear. We are corrupted by sin yet his mercy and grace redeems us when we live as he teaches. Stop, look and listen to the call of the one true savior who can give eternal life.

MY STRUGGLE

As the day approaches for the implementation of the mission, I'm dogged by evil. For every positive thought, there are multiple evil ones. The warring is so real that I frequently pause to evaluate. Firm I yet stand and devout I shall remain to the true spirit in me that has been with me since my youth. The voice which has guided and protected me these long years has always been a thought away. I doubt not my walk yet I entertain the evil whispers that are constantly there to tempt me as flesh will do. Whereas in my youth I may have succumbed to some of these evil whispers, but as a man, I'm astonished the evil persists. I know what evil is in all of its disguises because my spiritual faith and walk acts as my radar, my warning system, whenever evil comes neigh. If you don't have a warning system, the evil prevails and enters to carry out the sin of the one who sent it. Sin is evil which causes destruction and then death.

The opposite of evil is love, not hate, because evil and hate are one and the same. Love is life more abundantly and everlasting. Love inspires and supports hope and optimism. Love creates compassion and concern, uplifts and binds. As I began this writing, my spirit was burdened. As I write, the understanding comes and the burden is lifted. Job was an inspiration to us all. He was attacked in the most unbelievable manner because of his spirituality. Unlike most of us, or the disciples crossing to the other side during the storm with Jesus, Job's faith and knowledge was unshakable. We have seen miracles and signs of miracles. We have been brought through many trials and tribulations, none on the level of Job, yet we readily doubt when crisis arise. The disciples were with the master, "the master," the creator of this and all worlds, saw him perform "miracles" their minds could not conceive. Yet, a storm and a boat made them doubt. Isn't it ironic, the very things those men used to their lives profession, fishing and boating, the enemy used to make them doubt. The master, after being awakened, said to the wind, "cease," and the wind ceased. The master said to the water, "be still," and the water obeyed. I'm amazed when I ask a dog to sit. These disciples were a warning to us that without the armour of God, walking constantly in his word, we too would forever reap the rewards of them and all the "doubting Thomases."

Therefore, I throw out all doubt and apprehension this moment forward. The battle is I turn back in my favor against the evil that attack me as I try to do the good of my Lord. The battle raged a day and a night but this morning, I stand on the promise of my savior. I am the redeemed, I am the victor.

The battles have raged and victories have been consistent. I'm still here. Here to fight through the obstacles placed before me to hinder my work for the Lord. The carnal man has been revealed and mostly purged by prayer and submission. The rewards of the world have become merely instruments used to sustain me for my work as a servant of Christ. Whereas before the world was my all, Jesus has redefined my value system. Jesus is everything to me because only he can give both life on earth and everlasting life in Heaven. How blessed I am to be fed wisdom daily by Him because I seek His guidance. I write this so man will know spiritual growth does not come without struggle and sacrifice. To help with the struggles, this manual may offer ways to keep them focused on their individual missions. As a choir director manipulates the voices for different sounds, so too does the Holy Spirit with spiritual gifts. Many choir directors will tell you of the difficulties associated with allowing friends and families pressuring them into letting a "loved one" enter the choir who does not have the gift of song. Without knowing what your spiritual gifts are, you are destined to create and maintain disruption where you worship. You will not fulfill the mission your spirit was intended to bring forth.

So, this guide is an attempt at offering a path towards developing the spiritual gifts God placed in each of us so that He may be glorified and we, in the end, will be redeemed.

INTRODUCING THE MEN'S MINISTRY ACTION PLAN

1. We want to catch a fresh vision for our men's ministry.
2. Be challenged to think through and conceptualize:
   a) What is our vision for our men's ministry?
   b) What would we like to accomplish?
   c) How will we know whether we've accomplished our goals?
   d) What kind of men do we want to produce?
3. Learn how to create momentum among men to be involved in the men's ministry. We want input from each man as to what we should do and how to carry on this ministry.

We have been meeting for the men's fellowship breakfast the second Saturday of each month. The purpose has been to increase bonding opportunities for each man. The next step is to invite other men to join us for this fellowship and eventually invite them to our church. We will build our men's ministry by addressing and encouraging all of the above.

What follows are some helpful spiritual food ingredients for the growing spiritual man.

FOUR CORNERSTONES OF A SUCCESSFUL MEN'S MINISTRY

1) The senior pastor's enthusiastic support for a men's ministry.

2) A man passionate about reaching other men.

3) A committed leadership team.

4) We must be <u>purpose driven</u> rather than <u>event driven</u>.

STRONG WARRIORS ARMED TOGETHER
S-W-A-T

This is the title to be considered for our men's ministry. We will be a Christian centered ministry dedicated to uniting men through covenant relationships and to be pace setters honoring Jesus Christ in heart, home and harvest. Men's ministry, for the most part, is an undefined, undiscovered territory and only recently has begun to emerge in various models. It is apparent, however, that the primary goal of an effective men's ministry is to strategically help men transfer biblical truth into action by providing the necessary environments for them to make and keep their promises to Jesus Christ, their family, friends, churches, and communities. From this emerging men's ministry, there are basic principles that are being established.

The men's ministry, SWAT, is focused on facilitating relationships. It is a part of the church. Men gather in small support groups to encourage one another in their Christian walk and hold each other accountable to the biblical principles set forth for men. Clear goals are articulated to the men of the SWAT. These goals, biblically grounded and applicable to men, help men take ownership in the purpose of the men's ministry. SWAT offers a variety of entry points and opportunities for men to grow spiritually and to make relational commitments. This ministry honors and respects each man's spiritual journey, seeking ways to enhance his faith and commitment to God. Flexibility and variety of ministries allows room for the ministry to "keep in step with the spirit," trusting God to accomplish his purpose in a particular group of men. This ministry has a strong dependence on what God wants to accomplish in men's lives. SWAT offers the following opportunities:

1. Monthly brotherhood training;
2. Equipping seminars (father/son, marriage enrichment, leadership development);
3. Service projects; and
4. Activities (golfing, fishing, other recreational-social events).

At the heart of the SWAT is a commitment to encourage relationships that builds bridges. The scope of reconciliation includes unbeliever to God, man to himself, brother to brother, man to woman, husband to wife, wife to husband, parent to child, child to parent, church to church and people to people.

SWAT—FACT FILE

WHO?   For all men of the church and community

WHAT? A ministry to encourage relationships for men to God, family and church

WHEN? Monthly group meeting _____ at 7 pm.

TWO WOLVES

One evening, an old Cherokee told his grandson about a battle that goes on inside all people. He said, "My son! The battle is between two wolves inside us all.

One is evil. It is anger, envy, jealousy, sorrow, regret, greed, arrogance, self pity, guilt, resentment, inferiority, lies, false pride, superiority and ego.

The other is good. It is joy, love, peace, hope, serenity, humility, kindness, benevolence, empathy, generosity, truth, compassion and faith."

The grandson thought for a minute and then asked his grandfather, "Which wolf wins?"

The grandfather replied, "The one you feed."

WHAT IS SPIRITUAL LEADERSHIP?

While spiritual leadership involves many of the same principles as general leadership, spiritual leadership has certain distinctive qualities that must be understood and practiced if spiritual leaders are to be successful.

The spiritual leader's task is to move people from where they are to where God wants them to be. This is influence. Once spiritual leaders understand God's will, they make every effort to move their followers from following their own agendas to pursuing God's purposes. People who fail to move people to God's agenda have not led. They may have exhorted, cajoled, pleaded or bullied, but they will not have led until their people have adjusted their lives to God's will.

Spiritual leaders depend on the Holy Spirit. Spiritual leaders work within a paradox. For God calls them to do something that, in fact, only God can do. Ultimately, spiritual leaders cannot produce spiritual change in people; only the Holy Spirit can accomplish growth in others.

Spiritual leaders are accountable to God. Spiritual leadership necessitates an acute sense of accountability. Just as a teacher has not taught until students learn, leaders don't blame their followers when they don't do what they should do. Leaders don't make excuses. They assume their responsibility is to move people to do God's will.

Spiritual leaders can influence all people, not just God's people. God's agenda applies to the market place as well as the meeting place. Although spiritual leaders will generally move God's people to achieve God's purposes, God can use them to exert significant Godly influence upon unbelievers.

Spiritual leaders work from God's agenda. The greatest obstacle to effective spiritual leadership is people pursuing their own agendas rather than seeking God's will. Too often, people assume that along with the role of leader comes the responsibility of determining what should be done. They develop aggressive goals. They dream grandiose dreams. They cast grand visions. They then pray and ask God to join them in their agenda and bless their efforts. That's not what spiritual leaders do. They seek God's will, then, marshal their people to pursue God's plan.

Psalm 46:10—Be Still and Know That I *Am* GOD

Luke 6:27—"But I say to you who hear: Love your enemies, do good to those who hate you, 28 bless those who curse you, and pray for those who spitefully use you.

Leviticus 19:18—You shall not take vengeance, nor bear any grudge against the children of your people, but you shall love your neighbor as yourself: I *am* the LORD.

Psalm 46:1—God *is* our refuge and strength, a very present help in trouble.

Psalm 40:4—Blessed *is* that man who makes the LORD his trust, and does not respect the proud, or such as turn aside to lies.

5 — Many, O LORD, my God, *are* Your wonderful works
Which You have done;
And Your thoughts toward us
Cannot be recounted to You in order;
If I would declare and speak *of them,*
They are more than can be numbered.

6 — Sacrifice and offering you did not desire;
My ears you have opened.
Burnt offering and sin offering you did not require.

7 — Then I said, "Behold, I come;
In the scroll of the book it is written of me.

8 — I delight to do your will, O my God,
And your law *is* within my heart.

9 — I have proclaimed the good news of righteousness
In the great assembly;
Indeed, I do not restrain my lips,
O LORD, You yourself know.

10 — I have not hidden your righteousness within my heart;
I have declared your faithfulness and your salvation;
I have not concealed your loving kindness and your truth
From the great assembly.

11 — Do not withhold Your tender mercies from me, O LORD;
Let Your loving kindness and Your truth continually preserve me.

12 — For innumerable evils have surrounded me;
My iniquities have overtaken me, so that I am not able to look up;
They are more than the hairs of my head;
Therefore my heart fails me.

13 — Be pleased, O LORD, to deliver me;
O LORD, make hast to help me!

14 — Let them be ashamed and brought to mutual confusion
Who seek to destroy my life?
Let them be driven backward and brought to dishonor
Who wish me evil?

15 — Let them be confounded because of their shame,
Who say to me, "Aha, aha!"

16 — Let all those who seek You rejoice and be glad in You;
Let such as love your salvation say continually,

17 — But I *am* poor and needy;
Yet the LORD thinks upon me.
You *are* my help and my deliverer;
Do not delay, O my God.

James 1:19—My dear brothers, take note of this: Everyone should be quick to listen, slow to speak and slow to become angry,

20— for man's anger does not bring about the righteous life that God desires.

21— Therefore, get rid of all moral filth and the evil that is so prevalent, and humbly accept the word planted in you, which can save you.

22— Do not merely listen to the word, and so deceive yourselves. Do what it says.

SOME THINGS WE NEED TO REALIZE ABOUT OUR RELATIONSHIP WITH GOD AND OUR TALENTS

A. God has brought us out of a life of sin. We belong to Him.
   I Peter 1:18-19
   I Corinthians 6:19-20

B. We are God's bond servants
   Romans 6:16-18

C. God has entrusted us with various gifts or abilities that he expects us to use to his glory.
   I Corinthians 12:4-7
   Ephesians 4:11-13

D. We are stewards, given the responsibility to wisely use God's wealth given to our care.
   Luke 12:42-43
   I Peter 4:10

Remember! We must understand who we are so we can be affective for the body of Christ.

WAYS TO PRAISE THE LORD

1) Praise which can be heard
   Psalms 66:8, 17; 98:4; Acts 16:25
   There doesn't seem to be any Bible evidence that any praised the Lord silently in their hearts. It was always vocal and could be heard.

2) Praise the Lord with shouting
   Psalms 47:1; 35:27; 95:1
   There are many passages where the psalmist urged everyone to shout unto the Lord with the voice of victory.

3) Praise him with singing
   Psalm 47:6
   There are countless scriptures that show singing as one of the main forms of praise.

4) Praise your Lord with thanksgiving
   Psalms 69:30; 50:23; Jonah 2:9
   Next to singing praise, thanksgiving is the expression most understood. "In everything give thanks," the Apostle Paul exhorts in Ephesians 5:18-20.

5) Praise with clapping hands
   Psalms 47:1, 98:8
   In every area of life, clapping the hands is an expression of approval, excitement and pure joy.

6) Praise God with the Dance
   Psalms 30:1; 149:3; 150:4
   Dancing, as described by the psalmist, was more of a rejoicing jump than one of grace. "David danced before the Lord with all of his might," II Samuel 6:14.

7) Praise Him by falling prostrate before him
   Neh 8:6

HINDRANCES OF PRAISE AND WORSHIP

1) No spiritual imagination produced by the word to relate to.
2) Unforgiveness
3) Distractions, lies, unbelief, distrust produced by satanic influences in the mind
4) Worldliness, laziness
5) Lack of knowledge
6) Fear of man. Fear is a lie of the enemy.
7) Lack fellowship with the Father. No fellowship—no praise.
8) An unrighteous consciousness (Psalm 30:11-12)

ATTITUDE OPPOSITE OF PRAISE

1) Murmuring and complaining (Phil 2:14)
2) Unthankfulness (II Tim 3:1-2)
3) Refusing to recognize God (Romans 1:21-28)
4) If praise in Psalm 22 is a form of seeking God, then absence of praise in a believer means he is seeking something else and not God.

Developing a Wholesome Tongue
"A wholesome tongue is a tree of life . . . . (Proverbs 15:4)"

HINDRANCES TO DEVELOPING A WHOLESOME TONGUE

Lying Tongue—
"The Lord detests lying lips, but He delights in men who are truthful."
(Proverbs 12:22)
    Four forms of lying:
- Deceitfulness
- Half-truths
- Exaggerating
- Flattery (insincere compliment to gain favor)

Confession:
- For my mouth will speak truth; wickedness is an abomination to my lips. All the words of my mouth are with righteousness; nothing crooked or perverse is in them (Proverbs 8:7-8)

Hasty Tongue—
"Do you see a man who speaks in haste? There is more hope for a fool than him." (Proverbs 29:20)

Confession
- Let every man be swift to hear, slow to speak, slow to wrath. (James 1:19)

Dividing Tongue—
"These six things the Lord hates, yes, seven that are an abomination to Him . . . a false witness who speaks lies and one that sows discord among the brethren."
(Proverbs 6:16, 19)
  Ways to prevent strife with my words:
  - Don't start it
  - Don't repeat it
  - Don't spread it
  - Don't add to it
  Confession (I Corinthians 15:10)
  - Blessed are the peacemakers for they shall be called sons of God.

Boasting Tongue (Proverbs 27:2)
A boasting tongue will cause you to forget others and be very critical of someone else.
  Confession
  - By the grace of God I am what I am.

Self Depreciation Tongue (Exodus 4:10)
When you allow the enemy to trick you to do or say something that is not of God. Putting yourself down is called self-depreciation. You are simply rejecting yourself.
  Confession
  - I will reject the spirit of inadequacy. (Luke 8:30)

Slandering Tongue (Psalms 101:5)
Whoso privily slandereth his neighbor, him will I cut off; him that hath a high look and a proud heart, will not I suffer.
  Confession (Philippians 4:8)
  - I refuse to be a slanderer.

Gossiping Tongue (Proverbs 18:8)
The words of a talebearer are as wounds, and they go down into the innermost parts of the belly.
  Confession (Psalm 19:14)
  - Let the words of my mouth and the meditation of my heart be acceptable in thy sight, O Lord.

MARKS OF MATURITY

Measuring our spiritual growth

True Christianity forces us to face ourselves honestly. Christian maturity comes gradually as the following "heart issues" are resolved. Below are several *measuring rods* by which we may gauge spiritual growth.

"MEASURING RODS"
Maturity is measured by the following:

1. By how well we get along with others (John 17:21). Encompassed within this are all the following:
2. By how much contentment we have learned (Philippians 4:11-12; I Timothy 6:6).
3. By how well we rule our spirit and control our emotions—love or hate (Proverbs 16:32)
4. By how well we control our tongue. Most sins are committee with the tongue (James 3:2).
5. By how much we have dealt with pride and all other conflicts (Romans 12:3).
6. By how much patience we possess—all rashness and criticism subdued (Proverbs 18:13, Isaiah 32:4).
7. By how steadfast we are—no up and down, but constant "at all seasons" (Acts 20:18).

8. By how holy we are. Great ministry without *character* is of little worth (Matthew 7:20-23).
9. By how much of a servant's spirit we have. Humility is the mark of greatness (Mark 10:43-45).
10. By our attitudes toward authority. Bad attitudes reveal defiance toward the Lord (Ezekiel 3:7).
11. By how much we have mastered our thought life. Every battle is won or lost in Our mind (I Peter 1:13).
12. By how discreetly we handle finances. Money involves conscience and character (Luke 16:10-11).
13. By how much we have learned to *stop* saying, "it's not fair" (Genesis 45:5-8, 50:20).
14. By how much gratitude we have. Thankfulness is the key to victory (Eph. 5:20, I Thessalonians 5:18).
15. By how much we realize we do *not* know. The immature have all the answers (I Corinthians 8).
16. By how well we handle rejection—by how much understanding and forgiveness we have (Acts 5:41).
17. By how well we respond to painful delays—a proof of how far down our roots go (Psalm 40:1-2, Isa. 64:4)
18. By how well we handle personal failure or looking like a failure (I Samuel 30:6, Isaiah 49:4).
19. By how well we cope with the loss of something (Job 1:21).
20 By how well we handle hostility sent our way (Romans 12:17-21).
21. By how well we manage success! Do we continue to depend on God? (Deuteronomy 8:11-14).
22. By how much wisdom we accumulate. Wisdom is the principal thing (Proverbs 4:7, Luke 2:52).
23. By how much love we possess. Love it totally unselfish and the bond of perfectness (Colossians 3:14).
24. By how responsible and reliable we are, and by how much we fear the Lord (Nehemiah 7:2).
25. By how well we manage our time. Wasting time is wasting life. (Psalm 90:12, Ephesians 5:15-17)
26. By our attitude toward fallen brothers and sisters—cleansed of an *"I told you so"* Attitude (Galatians 6:1).
27. By how well we know ourselves, even as God knows us (I Corinthians 13:12), and by how much hypocrisy has been purged from our hearts (Matthew 7:1-5)? Hypocrisy is self-blindness.

TEMPTATION

Do I have the power to resist overwhelming temptation?"

What are some steps I can take to resist temptation?

What do I do when I fail?

Standing Scriptures

Proverbs: 25:28 "He that hath no rule over his own spirit is like a city that is broken down and without walls."

I Corinthians 10:13 "There hath no temptation taken you but such as is common to man: but God is faithful, who will not suffer you to be tempted above that ye are able; but will with the temptation also make a way to escape, that ye may be able to bear it."

Hebrews 2:18 "For in the He Himself hath suffered being tempted, He is able to succor them that are tempted."

Hebrews 4:15 "For we have not an high priest which cannot be touched with the feelings of our infirmities; but was in all points tempted like as we are, yet without sin."

James 1:2-3 "My brethren, count it all joy when ye fall into divers temptations; knowing this, that the trying of your faith worketh patience."

James 1:12-14 "Blessed is the man that endureth temptation: for when he is tried, he shall receive the crown of life, which the Lord hath promised to them that love him. Let no man say when he is tempted, I am tempted of God: for God cannot be tempted with evil, neither tempted He any man; But every man is tempted, when he is drawn away of his own lust, and enticed."

II Peter 2:9 "The Lord knoweth how to deliver the godly out of temptations, and to reserve the unjust unto the Day of Judgment to be punished."

Proverbs 16:32 "He that is slow to anger is better than the might; and he that ruleth his spirit than he that taketh the city."

TEMPTATION

*Experiencing Temptation
    Why is it so easy to give in to temptations? (Genesis 3:1-7)

Temptation is part of a crafty plan that appeals to our natural desires in attempt to separate us from God.

Temptation is an invitation to live a self-serving life that leads to rebellion against God.

Temptation feeds off our own tendency toward self-reliance.

Temptation is subtle; what if offers may seem harmless at first glance.

Temptation often hits hardest in our areas of weakness.

Temptation can strike any area of life.

*Resisting Temptation
    How can we resist temptations? (Genesis 3:1-7)

Resistance begins with being aware of temptation when it strikes.

Resist immediately; any delay makes it more difficult.

Have a plan for resisting temptation.

Remember that temptation to seemingly harmless sins can lead to harmful consequences.

Realize that temptation, in itself, is not a sin.

Do not be surprised by temptation at unlikely places.

"Lead us not"—
  Relevant, Spectacular, Powerful—Jesus' Purpose

INTEGRITY

The importance of Integrity

Psalm 7:8, "The Lord shall judge the people; Judge me, O Lord, according to my righteousness, and according to my integrity within me."

Here, David is asking God to judge him according to his righteousness and his integrity. Ask yourself this question, if you were standing before God today, and you asked God to judge you according to your righteousness and your integrity, how would you do? Would God be proud of you, would you be proud of yourself, or would you be ashamed, do you think that you have a great deal of work left to build your integrity?

The **definition of Integrity** in the Hebrew, the word integrity meant completeness, moral innocence, or perfection; the exact opposite of compromise.

Why is your Integrity important?
1. It defines to others who you are. When someone thinks of you, inevitably, they will think about whether or not you have integrity. People want to know if you're for real.
2. It determines how you will react in certain situations. When you are faced with circumstances where you have choice to either do right or do wrong, your integrity, or lack of it, will determine what you do.
3. It demonstrates your spiritual condition. If you have no integrity, then you have a spiritual problem, because God wants us to be righteous, to have integrity.
4. If you lack it, it can damage your testimony. If someone knows that you have no integrity, they will certainly not listen to you when you share the Gospel with them.

Business people / Christians

1. It pleases God. **I Chronicles 29:17,** "I know also, my God, that thou test the heart, and have pleasure in uprightness. As for me, in the uprightness of my heart I have willingly offered all these things; and now with joy I have seen your people, who are present here to offer willingly to you."

What will Integrity do for me?

1. It blesses Me. **Proverbs 20:7,** "The just man walk in his integrity, his children are bless after him."
2. It judges Me. **Job 31:6** "Let me be weighed in an even balance, that God may know mine integrity. God will judge us according to our righteousness and integrity. **Psalms 7:8** that we have already read."
3. It protects me. **Psalms 25:21,** "Let integrity and rightness preserve me. Integrity will protect us as we venture through life. Some people spend so much time worrying about what they said to whom, or how they acted in a certain situation because they have no integrity. A person with integrity never has to worry about what story he told to whom, because he will always be telling the same story. His integrity will protect him.
4. It guides me. **Proverbs 11:3,** "The integrity of the upright shall guide them. Our integrity will guide our steps through life. We will not have to worry what to do in certain situations, because we always trust in God who will direct us.

How do I get it?

1. You pursue it with all your heart. Spend your lives seeking integrity. Desire it as you make every decision. Base your life on it. Base your walk on it. Be able to say, like David did in **Psalms 26:1,** "Judge me, O Lord, for I have walked in mine integrity, we will not slide backward, we will not lose our direction.
2. You protect it with all your heart. Why, because you can easily lose your integrity. If you are not careful, if you don't seek it, and protect it daily, you may walk away from it.
   a. Your daily walk
   b. Studying His word
   c. Prayer time

3. You practice it with all your heart. In every decision, in every situation you find yourself in, act with integrity.
4. You pray for it. Seek God earnestly that he will let you be a man or woman of integrity. Pray that God would use you to be an example to others of what integrity is all about.

Conclusion

- Soon, whether you are just getting started in this life or a person facing or have already retired, you should live a life of integrity. If you base your life on God's Word and His principles, you will have a life of integrity that can change the world. If the people in your neighborhood, in your office, in your family, know you as a man of integrity, how much easier will it be for you to share the Gospel with them than if you were known to lack integrity? Having integrity is our choice, let's choose to do right.

REMEMBER

What you say should always be what you do because that reflects WHO you really are!

TEACHINGS ABOUT LIFE'S PROBLEMS

- Adultery
  Matthew 5:27-32
- Adversity
  Matthew 10:16-39
- Anger
  Matthew 5:22-24
- Anxiety
  Matthew 6:19-34
- Conceit
  Luke 18:9-14
- Covetousness
  Mark 7:21-23
- Crime
  Matthew 15:17-20
- Death
  John 11:25-26
- Depravity
  John 3:19-21
- Divorce
  Mark 10:2-12
- Doubt
  Matthew 14:28-31
- Drunkenness
  Luke 21:34-36
- Excuses
  Luke 14:-15-24
- Extravagance
  I Timothy 6:7-12
- Fault finding
  Matthew 7:1-5

- Fear
  Luke 12:5
- Flesh
  Romans 13:14
- Greed
  Luke 12:15-31
- Hatred / Enemies
  Matthew 5:43-48
- Hypocrisy
  Matthew 23:27-28
- Judging
  Matthew 7:1
- Lip service
  Matthew 7:21
- Lust
  Mark 4:18-19
- Self-exaltation
  Luke 14:11
- Self-righteousness
  Luke 18:11-12
- Sin
  John 8:34-36
- Submission
  I Peter 2:13-17
- Swearing
  Colossians 3:8
- Tribulation
  John 16:33
- Worldliness
  I John 2:15-17

WHERE TO LOOK WHEN

- Afraid
  Psalm 34:4
  Matthew 10:28
  II Timothy 1:7
  Hebrews 13:5-6
- Anxious
  Psalm 46
  Matthew 6:19-34
  Philippians 4:6
  I Peter 5:6-7
- Backsliding
  Psalm 51
  I John 1:4-9
- Bereaved
  Matthew 5:4
  II Corinthians 1:3-4
- Bitter—Critical
  I Corinthians 13
- Conscious of sin
  Proverbs 28:13
- Defeated
  Romans 8:31-39
- Depressed
  Psalm 34
- Disaster threatens
  Psalm 91
  Psalm 118:5-6
  Luke 8:22-25
- Discouraged
  Psalm 23

  Psalm 42:6-11
  Psalm 55:22
  Matthew 5:11-12
  II Corinthians 4:8-18
  Philippians 4:4-7
- Doubting
  Matthew 8:26
  Hebrews 11
- Facing crisis
  Psalm 121
  Matthew 6:25-34
  Hebrews 11
- Faith fails
  Psalm 42:5
  Hebrews 11
- Friends fail
  Psalm 41:9-13
  Luke 17:3-4
  Romans 12:14, 17, 19, 21
  II Timothy 4:16-18
- Leaving home
  Psalm 121
  Matthew 10:16-20
- Lonely
  Psalm 23
  Hebrews 13:5, 6
- Needing God's protection
  Psalm 27:1-3
  Psalm 91
  Philippians 4:19

- Needing guidance
  Psalm 32:8
  Proverbs 3:5, 6
- Needing peace
  John 14: 1-4
  John 16:33
  Romans 5:1-5
  Philippians 4:6, 7
- Needing rules for life
  Romans 12
- Overcome
  Psalm 6
  Romans 8:31-39
  I John 1: 4-9
- Prayerful
  Psalm 4
  Psalm 42
  Luke 11:1-13
  John 17
  I John 5:14-15
- Protected
  Psalm 18:1-3
  Psalm 34:7
- Sick—In pain
  Psalm 38
  Matthew 26:39
  Romans 5:3-5
  II Corinthians 12: 9-10
  I Peter 4:12-13, 19
- Sorrowful
  Psalm 51
  Matthew 5:4
  John 14
  II Corinthians 1:3-4
  I Thessalonians 4:13-18
- Tempted
  Psalm 1
  Psalm 139:23-24
  Matthew 26:41
  I Corinthians 10:12-14

- Philippians 4:8
  James 4:7
  II Peter 2:9, 3:17
- Thankful
  Psalm 100
  I Thessalonians 5:18
  Hebrews 13:15
- Traveling
  Psalm 121
- Trouble, in
  Psalm 16:31
  John 14:1-4
  Hebrews 7:25
- Weary
  Psalm 90
  Matthew 11:28-30
  I Corinthians 15:58
  Galatians 6:9-10
- Worried
  Matthew 6:19-34
  I Peter 5:6-7

SPIRITUAL GIFTS

Spiritual Gifts are given so the Holy Spirit can work through the gifted believer to spiritually benefit other believers in the body of Christ and reach out to those who are not believers.

Spiritual Gifts	**vs.**	**Responsibilities**

Spiritual Gifts are extraordinary abilities that the spirit gives to a believer to build up the church. Even though such attributes as faith, teaching, and giving are considered gifts, all Christians are exhorted to develop these traits.

Some Christians are given

But all believers are called

Divine Wisdom (I Corinthians 12:8)

To live wisely (Romans 16:19; Ephesians 5:15; Col. 4:5)

Extraordinary Faith (I Cor. 12:9)

To walk by faith (II Cor. 5:7) and abound in faith (II Cor. 8:7); to take of the shield of faith (Eph. 6:16) and pursue faith (I Tim 6:12, II Tim 2:22)

Special Teaching Gifts (I Cor 12:28; Rom 12:7)

To teach others the truths of God (Matt 28:20; II Tim 2:2, 24)

Supernatural Ability to Help (I Cor. 28)

To serve one another in love (Gal. 5:13) and to minister to others Romans 12:7)

The Ability to Give Liberally (Rom. 12:8)

To give "not grudgingly or of necessity" but cheerfully (II Cor. 9:7)

Divine Power to Show Mercy (Rom. 12:8)

To be merciful (Luke 6:36; James 2:13)

SPIRITUAL GIFTS
(TEST)

1. Who gets the gifts of the spirit (at least one)? I Cor. 12:7

2. What are the gifts? List them.
   I Cor. 12:8-11, 28
   Romans 12:6-8
   Ephesians 4:11
   I Peter 4:9-11

3. When were we given our gifts? Ephesians 4:8

4. Why were we given our gifts: I Cor. 12:7

5. Are all Christians supposed to be alike?
   I Cor. 12:21-31

6. What is even better than song spiritual gifts? I Cor. 12:31—Chapter 13

7. Prayerfully go through your list of the gifts, asking God to show you your gift and how to use it.

THE GIFT OF EXHORTATION

Colossians 3:12-17

God's plan is to equip believers with spiritual gifts so that kingdom work can be carried out according to his plan. The gift of exhortation has these characteristics:

1) A goal of spiritual maturity in others.

2) Discernment of root causes.

3) Skill in solving problems.

FRUIT OF THE SPIRIT

"Fruit of the Spirit" is a biblical term that sums up the nine visible attributes of a true Christian's life. Galatians 5:22-23, these attributes are: "but the fruit of the spirit is love, joy, peace, long suffering, gentleness, goodness, faith, meekness, and temperance; against such there is no law." Paul's final comment on the "Fruit of the Spirit" indicates that there are no restrictions to the life style indicated. Christians, in fact, ought to practice these virtues repeatedly; They will never discover a law prohibiting them from living according to these principles.

We learn from these scriptures that these "fruit" are not selected individually. Rather, the "Fruit of the Spirit" is one nine fold "fruit" that characterizes all who truly walk in the Holy Spirit. Collectively, all Christians should be producing these "fruit" in their new lives with Christ.

"Fruit of the Spirit"—The nine biblical attributes, is a physical manifestation of a Christian's transformed life. In order to mature as believers, we should study and understand the attributes of the nine fold fruits:

Meekness: Is a word that is often misunderstood by those who read The Bible. It does not mean one is spineless or ineffective. Meekness means "teachable." A person who is unteachable lacks an attitude of confidence. **II Corinthians 3:5,** "not that we are sufficient of ourselves to think anything as of ourselves; but our sufficiency is of God." Meekness is an encouraging fruit. It encourages positive results. Meekness is coachable and listens with humility (II Corinthians 10:1, Colossians 3:12).
Titus 3:2, "to speak evil of no man, to be no brawlers, but gentle, showing all meekness unto all men."

Galatians 6:1, "brethren, if a man be over taken in a fault, ye which are spiritual, restore such a one in the spirit of meekness; considering thyself, lest thou also be tempted."

Ephesians 4:2, "with all lowliness and meekness, with long suffering, for bearing one another in love."

I Timothy 6:11, "but thou, O man of God, flee these things; and follow after righteousness, Godliness, faith, patience, meekness."

James 3:13, "who is a wise man and endured with knowledge among you? Let him show out of a good conversation (conduct) his works with meekness and wisdom."

Temperance (Self-control): Is the final fruit of the spirit mentioned in Galatians 5:22-23. Temperance means self-control. Temperance is a guarding fruit. By exercising self-control, we control and guard our results. The more you study to be spiritual, the more control we have over our actions and thoughts. **II Peter 1:5-7,** "but also for this reason, giving all diligence, add to your faith virtue, to virtue knowledge, to knowledge self-control, to perseverance Godliness, to Godliness brotherly love." Virtue means moral excellence, merit and good quality. **I Corinthians 9:25,** "and every man that strive for mastery is temperate (self-control) in all things. Now they do it to obtain a corruptive crown but we are incorruptible.

Self-control guards results:

1. Love—activate by doing
2. Joy—encourages with excitement
3. Peace—guards by quieting
4. Longsuffering—(patience) forbears and endures by doing
5. Gentleness—wins others by encouraging
6. Goodness—guards by ministering
7. Faith—(believing) appropriates by doing
8. Meekness—encourages positive results
9. Temperance—(self control) guards results

As we review the meaning of the nine fruit of the spirit, we must make the appropriate changes if we want to operate in these areas. When we surrender, our spirits will be fed and watered allowing us to grow and produce a bountiful harvest.

Self-control—is what causes others to trust you!

Fruit—is produced to help benefit others!

Help Wanted
Everyone can get involved!

Help Wanted
Everyone can get Involved!

_____

_____

We are preparing to serve the Lord at a greater level of excellence and we want to include you. We believe that we should be developing members to move from membership to serving in ministry.

Below are listed areas of service ministry. Please indicate where you are willing to serve your church.

☐ Evangelist/ Outreach	☐ Church beautification (outside)
☐ Music Department	☐ Youth Choir
☐ Children's Ministry	☐ Public Relations
☐ Women's Ministry	☐ Website/ Technology ministry
☐ Church beautification (inside)	☐ Bus outreach
☐ Photography	☐ Host/Hostess
☐ Video Taping	☐ Greeters
☐ Fine Arts	☐ Building maintenance
☐ Drama	☐ Pastoral care
☐ Clerical & Office volunteer	☐ Pastoral care
☐ Tape ministry	☐ Security/ Parking
☐ Mass choir	☐ Mercy/Hospital
☐ Sound Tech	☐ Bookstore

- ☐ Singles ministry
- ☐ Marriage ministry
- ☐ Greeting card ministry
- ☐ Membership services
- ☐ Newsletter
- ☐ Prayer ministry
- ☐ Praise team
- ☐ Musician
- ☐ Special events team
- ☐ Children's choir
- ☐ Phone encouragement

Name:_____

Address:_____

Phone: (day)_____(evening)_____

Email address:_____

Member of team:_____Ambassador_____Dan_____Joshua_____Lev

Comments/Questions:_____

_____

THE MINISTRY OF HELPS

The **Ministry of Helps** is one of the most needed ministries in the Body of Christ. For without it many other ministries could not function or even exist. The person with this ministry has an eye to see what needs to be done.

You do not have to be in the forefront or to be recognized to function. The person with this ministry is mostly **"Helpers"** or **"Armour bearers"** (servants), and they are in the Body of Christ to assist and bring increase and support. This ministry can increase your vision for your ultimate call in God.

If those in the **Ministry of Helps** such as ushers, yardman, tape ministry, music ministry, praise / worship team, announcer, Sunday school teachers, public relations, hospitality, secretaries, office helpers, and cleaning persons, etc; take their jobs seriously, they pray about every decision they make in all that they do. We need those that wait on tables; ushers and yardmen to keep the grounds looking good. These are servants of the ministry. **Jesus considered himself a servant of the Father.**

Those named above are servants on a different level of authority. Jesus did not come to this earth to be ministered to, but to minister and to give His life as a ransom. He gave His life and we must also present our bodies a living sacrifice to God **(Romans 12:1)**.

It is our desire to relate to you that you can be totally fulfilled operating in the **Ministry of Helps**, Knowing that this is the vehicle that will take you to your next level of ministry in the Body of Christ. We started out in the **Ministry of Helps** working as a doorkeeper (usher, hospitality) and loved it, and still working in whatever capacity we're needed.

"Helps" means the ability to render service. The person with this gift likes to help with projects. He/She likes to work behind the scenes. The person with this kind of gift can serve others without feeling used. He/She has an eye to see what needs to be done.

- He/She is always doing something for someone.
- He/She likes to be involved in different activities.
- He/She likes to follow the leader.
- He/She has a burden for other people's needs to finds ways to help them.
- He/She is more attracted to the needy.

No ministry can function without helpers. God brings these helpers along to encourage, to build, to support and to bring increase. They share and help lift the heavy loads from God's people.

1) Elders in the church were men who were mature both _____ and _____.

2) Where is the scripture where the first deacons were chosen?

3) What does I Corinthians 12:4-7 say?

4) Name some servants working in the **"Ministry of Helps."**

10 THINGS CHRISTIANS CAN DO EVERYDAY . . .

1. **TREAT OTHERS AS YOU WOULD HAVE THEM TREAT YOU**:
    Treat other people in the manner that you want them to treat you.
    This is a hallmark of Christianity. Be kind to people, even when
    they are unkind to you. That way, you set an example for them. You
    become a representative of the Christian faith.

    "So, in everything, do to others what you would have them do to
    you" **Matthew 7:12** (NIV)

2. **HELP PEOPLE:**
    In Matthew 25:34-40, Jesus tells us that we are to give food to
    those who are hungry, give clothes to people who need them,
    provide shelter for people who have none, visit people who are sick
    and give comfort to people who are in prison.

3. DON'T WORRY:
    Do your best. Deal with life's problems but don't worry. Instead,
    have faith in Jesus that all things will work out in the way they need
    to work out.

    "Who of you by worrying can add a single hour to his life?"—Jesus,
    as quoted in **Matthew 6:27** (NIV)

4. **READ THE BIBLE:**
    If you read The Bible for about 10 to 20 minutes a day, you can finish
    the four gospels—The books for Matthew, Mark, Luke and John—
    in one month. The four gospels describe the life and teachings of
    Jesus, the son of God.

5. **GIVE THANKS AND BE JOYFUL:**
"Be joyful always; pray continually; give thanks in all circumstances, for this is God's will for you in Christ Jesus."—**I Thessalonians 5:16-18** (NIV)

6. **PRAY:**
"This, then, is how you should pray:
Our father in heaven, hallowed be your name, Your kingdom come, Your will be done on Earth as it is in heaven. Give us today our daily bread. Forgive us our debts, as we also have forgiven our debtors. And lead us not into temptation, but deliver us from evil."
—Jesus, explaining how people should pray, as quoted in **Matthew 6:9-13** (NIV).

7. **FORGIVE YOUR ENEMIES:**
"For if you forgive men when they sin against you, your Heavenly Father will also forgive you. But if you do not forgive men their sins, your father will not forgive your sins."
—**Matthew 6:14-15**

8. **BE CAREFUL WHAT YOU SAY ABOUT OTHER PEOPLE:**
"But I tell you that men will have to give account on the Day of Judgment for every careless word they have spoken. For by your words you will be acquitted, and by your words you will be condemned."—Jesus, as quoted in **Matthew 12:36-37**

9. **KNOW THE WORD OF GOD AND USE IT EACH DAY:**
If you read the four gospels—Matthew, Mark, Luke and John—you will see many examples of how Christians should act.

"Therefore everyone who hears these words of mine and puts them into practice is like a wise man who built his house on the rock."—**Matthew 7:24**

10. **ENCOURAGE OTHERS TO READ THE BIBLE:**
If you have found peace and salvation in The Bible, share it with others—tell people. Write a letter, or create a web site. Encourage other to read The Bible. Encourage family members and friends to attend church with you. Consider giving bibles as gifts to others.

"Therefore go and make disciples of all nations, baptizing them in the name of the Father and of the Son and of the Holy Spirit, and teaching them to obey everything I have commanded you. And surely I am with you always, to the very end of the age.—**Matthew 28:19-20**

"AM I MY BROTHER'S KEEPER?"

Genesis 4 : 9

INTRODUCTION

1. Perhaps one of the more thought-provoking questions in the Bible is that one asked by Cain:
   a. Cain had killed his brother because God had accepted Abel's offering, but not his own—**Gen 4:3-8**
   b. When the Lord inquired concerning Abel, Cain's response was:

   "Am I my brother's keeper?" (Gen 4:9)

2. This is a question we would do well to ask ourselves today . . .
   a. Are we our brother's keeper?
   b. Do we have a responsibility to watch out for and care for one another?

[When one turns to the New Testament, it becomes clear that the answer is in the affirmative. In fact, there are many passages which emphasize . . .]

I. OUR RESPONSIBILITIES TO ONE ANOTHER
   ### A. WE ARE TO "LOVE ONE ANOTHER"
   1. As commanded by Jesus—**John 13:34-35; 15:12, 17**
   2. As taught by Paul—**Ro 13:8, I Th 4:9**
   3. As instructed by Peter—**I Pe 1:22**

4. As stressed by John—**I John 3:11 (note v.12), 23; 4:7, 11-12; II John 5**

—But how are we to express such love? Other passages can provide the answer . . .

B. **HOW WE SHOW OUR LOVE FOR ONE ANOTHER**
1. We are to "receive one another"—**Ro 15:7**
2. We are to "edify another"—**Ro 14:19**
3. We are to "serve one another"—**Ga 5:13**
4. We are to "bear one another's burdens"—**Ga 6:1-2**
5. We are to be "forgiving one another"—**Ep 4:32**
6. We are to be "submitting to one another"—**Ep 5:21**
7. We are to "exhort one another"—**He 3:12-13**
8. We are to "consider one another"—**He 10:24-25**
9. We are to be "hospitable to one another"—**I Pe 4:8-10**

[In light of such "one another" passages, is there any doubt that we are to be our brother's keeper?

But how well are we doing? To stimulate our thinking and help us re-example how well we are fulfilling our obligations to one another, consider the following questions . . .]

II. <u>**EVALUATING OUR ROLE AS OUR BROTHER'S KEEPER**</u>
A. **WHEN ONE BECOMES A BROTHER** . . .
1. Do we **receive** them into the family of God, or ignore them?—**Ro 15:7**
   a. Are they properly assimilated in the family of the congregation?
   b. Do they remain on the fringe?
      —If we do not even know their names, we can be sure that they are failing as our brother's keeper!
2. Do we **edify** them, or put stumbling blocks in their way?—**Ro 14:19**
   a. As individuals, are we "body-builders", encouraging the members of the body?
   b. Or are we like a cancer, weakening the members of the body of Christ?
      1. By our own example
      2. By our words, attitudes, etc.

—It was said of Philemon that he refreshed the hearts of the brethren; do people say the same of us?

3. Do we **submit** to them, or arrogantly rule over them?—**Ep 5:21**
4. Do we **serve** them in love, or expect them to serve us?—**Ga 5:13**
5. Do we demonstrate **hospitality** to them?—**I Pe 4: 8-10**
   a. By visiting them in their need?
   b. By inviting them into your home (or accepting invitations to their home)?

B. **WHEN A BROTHER IS OVERTAKEN IN A FAULT** . . .
1. Do we even **consider** them?—**He 10:24-25**
   a. Are we even aware of whom they are?
   b. Are we ignorant of their problems? If so, why?
      1) Maybe it is because we don't assemble enough ourselves?
      2) We may "wonder about them," but that is not sufficient!
   c. Do they drift away, with no one making an effort to reach them?
2. Do we **exhort** them, lest they become hardened by sin?—**He 3:12-14**
   a. Or are we afraid to confront them, for fear of running them away?
      1) If we truly love them and approach them with humility, they are not likely to run away.
      2) If they do, they are running away from God, not you!
   b. Remember, such exhortation is to be daily! Perhaps we wait too long . . .
3. Are we willing to **bear their burdens**?—**Ga 6:1-2**
   a. So as to help them overcome and become stronger
   b. Or do we rather not be bothered?
4. Are we quick to **forgive** them when they repent?—**Ep 4:32**
   a. Fear of not being forgiven and accepted back into the family may keep some from repenting and returning to the fold
   b. Do we communicate a willingness to accept with open arms and offer complete forgiveness?

Conclusion

1. How we answer such questions may reveal how well or poorly we are . . .

a. Fulfilling our responsibility to be our brother's keeper
b. Living up to the one responsibility we have that includes all others: **to love one another as Christ loved us—John 13:34-35**

2. If we failed to be our brother's keeper, we need to . . .
   a. **Repent** of our lack of concern, our inactivity, or whatever has hindered us
   b. **Confess** our shortcomings in this area to God
   c. **Resolve** to apply with zeal these "on another" passages!

Are you your brother's keeper? Are you even identified with a congregation whereby you can be a working member who both cares for those in the family, and be cared for by them?

I hope this study has stimulated your thinking about responsibilities you have toward your brethren in Christ . . .

CHRISTIAN VIRTUES & CHARACTER

- **Abundant life**
  John 10:10
- **Citizenship**
  Romans 13:1-7
  Titus 3:1
- **Cleanliness**
  II Corinthians 7:1
- **Consecration**
  Romans 12:1-2
- **Contentment**
  Philippians 4:11-13
  I Timothy 6:6
- **Courage**
  Psalm 27:14
- **Diligence**
  Romans 12:11
- **Duty**
  Luke 20:21-25
- **Endurance**
  Luke 21:9-19
  II Timothy 2:3
- **Faith**
  Matthew 8:5-13
  Mark 11:22-24
- **Faithfulness**
  Matthew 25:23
- **Forgiveness**
  Mark 11:25-26
  Ephesians 4:31-32

- **Freedom**
  John 8:31-36
- **Fruitfulness**
  John 15:1-8
- **Godliness**
  Titus 2:11-14
- **Happiness**
  Matthew 5:3-12
- **Holiness**
  I Peter 1:13-16
- **Honesty**
  II Corinthians 8:21
- **Honor: Parents, others**
  Ephesians 6:1-3
  I Peter 2:17
- **Hope**
  I Peter 1:13
- **Humility**
  Luke 18:9-14
  Philippians 2:3-11
- **Joy**
  Luke 10:20
  John 15:11
- **Kindness**
  Colossians 3:12-13
- **Labor**
  John 9:4
- **Love**
  Luke 10:27
  I Corinthians 13

- **Obedience**
  John 14:15-24
  Acts 5:29
- **Overcoming**
  John 16:33
- **Patience**
  Hebrews 10:36
- **Peacefulness**
  John 14:27
  Romans 12:18
- **Perseverance**
  Mark 13:5-13
- **Prayer**
  Luke 11:1-13
  Ephesians 6:18
- **Pure thinking**
  Philippians 4:8
- **Purity**
  Matthew 5:27-32
  II Timothy 2:22
- **Reading the Bible**
  John 5:39
  Psalm 1:2
  Psalm 119:97
- **Resolution**
  Ephesians 6:10-18
- **Righteousness**
  Matthew 5:6
  Mathew 6:33
- **Sincerity**
  Philippians 1:9-10
- **Steadfastness**
  I Corinthians 15:58
- **Stewardship**
  I Corinthians 4:2
  II Corinthians 9:6-7
- **Temperance**
  I Thessalonians 5:6-8

- **Trust**
  Psalm 37:3-7
  Proverbs 3:5-6
- **Truth**
  John 14:6
  John 17:17
  Ephesians 4:14-15
- **Victory**
  I Corinthians 15:57
  I John 5:4
- **Watchfulness**
  Mark 13:34-37
- **Worship**
  John 4:23-24
- **Zeal**
  Romans 12:11

PASTOR VOICE

Standing Scriptures:

John 10: 1-5
Verse 1: Verily, verily, I say unto you, He that entereth not by the door into the sheepfold, but climbeth up some other way, the same is a thief and a robber.
Verse 2: But he that entereth in by the door is the shepherd of the sheep.
Verse 3: To him the porter openeth; and the sheep hear his voice; and he calleth his own sheep by name, and leadeth them out.
Verse 4: And when he putteth forth his own sheep, he goeth before them, and the sheep follow him; for they know his voice.
Verse 5: And a stranger will they not follow, but will flee from him: for they know not the voice of strangers.

John 10:27
Verse 27: My sheep, hear my voice, and I know them, and they follow me.
[Jesus expresses in these scriptures that sheep have the unique ability to distinguish the voice of "their" shepherd from that of other voices. Sheep will not follow the voices of strangers. Jesus states that His sheep will flee from the voice of strangers.

I Corinthians 14: 10-11
Verse 10: There are, it may be, so many kinds of voices in the world, and none of them is without signification.
Verse 11: Therefore if I know not the meaning of the voice, I shall be unto him that speaketh a barbarian, and he that speaketh shall be a barbarian unto me.

[In these scriptures, Paul addresses concerns by telling us there are many voice in the world and they all have an impact, as well as meaning. He declares that the problem is found in not distinguishing the varied meaning of many voices.]

I Peter 5:2-4
Verse 2: Feed the flock of God which is among you, taking the oversight thereof, not by constraint, but willingly; not for filthy lucre, but of a ready mind;
Verse 3: Neither as being lords over God's heritage, but being examples to the flock.
Verse 4: And when the chief Shepherd shall appear, ye shall receive a crown of glory that fadeth not away.

God speaks to us in our spirit where he lives; not in our minds.
Amos 8:11-12
Verse 11: Behold, the days come, saith the Lord GOD, that I will send a famine in the land, not a famine of bread, nor a thirst for water, but of hearing the words of the LORD;
Verse 12: And they shall wander from sea to sea, and from the north even to the east, they shall run to and fro to seek the word of the LORD, and shall not find it.

Mark 4:23-25
Verse 23: If any man have ears to hear, let him hear.
Verse 24: And he said unto them, Take heed what ye hear: with what measure ye mete, it shall be measured to you: and unto you that hear shall more be given.
Verse 25: For he that hath, to him shall be given: and he that hath not, from him shall be taken even that which he hath.

Luke 8:18
Verse 18: Take heed therefore how ye hear: for whosoever hath, to him shall be given: and whosoever hath not, from him shall be taken even that which he seemeth to have.

James 1:22
Verse 22: But be ye doers of the word, and not hearers only, deceiving your own selves.

Matthew 13:9-13
Verse 9: Who hath ears to hear, let him hear.
Verse 10: And the disciples came, and said unto him, Why speakest thou unto them in parables?
Verse 11: He answered and said unto them, Because it is given unto you to know the mysteries of the kingdom of heaven, but to them it is not given.
Verse 12: For whosoever hath, to him shall be given, and he shall have more abundance: but whosoever hath not, from him shall be taken away even that he hath.
Verse 13: Therefore speak I to them in parables: because they seeing see not; and hearing they hear not, neither do they understand.

Job 12:11
Verse 11: Doth not the ear try words? And the mouth taste this meat?

II Timothy 4:3-4
Verse 3: For the time will come when they will not endure sound doctrine; but after their own lusts shall they heap to themselves teachers, having itching ears;
Verse 4: And they shall turn away their ears from the truth, and shall be turned unto fables.

I Samuel 3:4-9
Verse 4: That the LORD called Samuel: and he answered, Here am I.
Verse 5: And he ran unto Eli, and said, Here am I: for thou calledst me. And he said, I called not; lie down again. And he went to lay down.
Verse 6: And the LORD called yet again, Samuel. And Samuel arose and went to Eli, and said, Here am I; for thou didst call me. And he answered, I called not, my son; lie down again.
Verse 7: Now Samuel did not yet know the LORD, neither was the word of the LORD yet revealed unto him.
Verse 8: And the LORD called Samuel again the third time. And he arose and went to Eli, and said, Here am I; for thou didst call me. And Eli perceived that the LORD had called the child.
Verse 9: Therefore Eli said unto Samuel, Go, lie down; and it shall be, if he call thee, that thou shalt say, Speak, LORD; for thy servant heareth. So Samuel went to lay down in his place.

LOSING THE HEART OF THE PASTOR

"The Bible says the race is not won by the swiftest, but those who endure unto the end, shall be saved. Endurance is one of the most important qualities in a believer's life. So many get a good start serving the Lord. Their excitement for the Lord's work is with great enthusiasm. They find a local church and meet new friends and grow very close to the Lord. They are so thrilled to serve in the house of God, as soon as the pastor makes mention of a task needing to be done, they swiftly perform the task. They are so eager at first, to do whatever the pastor hints that needs to be done. But in the process of time, they let any number of things stop them. Now, their once fast pace is slowed down.

LOSING THE HEART OF THE PASTOR

Standing Scriptures:

Matthew 16:18—I will build my church; and the gates of hell shall not prevail against it.

Acts 6:1—murmuring . . . Grecians against Hebrews, (KJV)

I Corinthians 1:11—It hath been declared unto me of you, my brethren, by them which are of the house of Chloe, that there are contentions among you. (KJV)

I Corinthians 11:18—For first of all, when ye come together in the church, I hear that there be divisions among you; and I partly believe it.

III John 1:9—but Diotrephes, who loveth to have the preeminence among them, receiveth us not.

II Timothy 3:6-8—For of this sort are they which creep into houses, and lead captive silly women laden with sins, led away with divers lusts, (7) Ever learning, and never able to come to the knowledge of the truth. (8) Now as Jannes and Jambres withstood Moses, so do these also resist the truth; men of corrupt minds, reprobate concerning the faith. (KJV)

II Timothy 4:14—Alexander the coppersmith did me much evil.

II Timothy 2:17—And their word will eat as doth a canker.

James 4:1—From whence come wars and fightings among you?

Ezekiel 34:17-19—And as for you, O my flock, thus said the Lord God, Behold, I judge between cattle and cattle, between the rams and the he goats. (18) Seemeth it a small thing unto you to have eaten up the good pasture, but ye must tread down with your feet the residue of your pastures? And to have drunk of the deep waters, but ye must foul the residue with your feet? (19) And as for my flock, they eat that which ye have trodden with your fee; and they drink that which ye have fouled with your feet.

Mark 14:27—And Jesus saith unto them, All ye shall be offended because of me this night for it is written, I will smite the shepherd, and the sheep shall be scattered.

Exodus 32:21-24—And Moses said unto Aaron, What did this people do unto thee, that thou hast brought so great a sin upon them? (22) And Aaron said, Let not the anger of my Lord wax hot; though knowest the people, that they are set on mischief. (23) For they said unto me, Make us gods, which shall go before us; for as for this Moses, the man that brought us up out of the land of Egypt, we wot not what is become of him. (24) And I said unto them, Whosoever hath any gold, let them break it off. So they gave it to me; then I cast it into the fire, and there came out this calf.

Numbers 12:1-2—And Miriam and Aaron spake against Moses because of the Ethiopian woman whom he had married; for he had married and Ethiopian woman. (2) And they said, Hath the Lord indeed spoken only by Moses? Hath he not spoken also by us? And the Lord heard it.

Numbers 16:1-3—Now Korah, the son of Izhar, the son of Kohath, the son of Levi, and Dathan and Abiram, the sons of Eliab, and On, the son of Peleth, sons of Reuben, took men; (2) and they rose up before Moses, with certain of the children of Israel, two hundred and fifty princes of the assembly, famous in the congregation, men of renown; (3) And they gathered themselves together against Moses and against Aaron, and said unto them, Ye take too much upon you, seeing all the congregation are holy, every one of them, and the Lord is among them: wherefore then lift ye up yourselves above the congregation of the Lord?

Numbers 16: 32-35—And the earth opened her mouth, and swallowed them up, and their houses, and swallowed them up, and their houses, and all the men that appertained unto Korah, and all their goods. They, and all that appertained to them, went down alive into the pit, and the earth closed upon them: and they perished from among the congregation. And all Israel that were round about them fled at the cry of them: for they said, Lest the earth swallow us up also. And there came out a fire from the Lord, and consumed the two hundred and fifty men that offered incense.

Numbers 16:41—But on the morrow all the congregation of the children of Israel murmured against Moses and against Aaron, saying, ye have killed the people of the Lord.

Numbers 16:49—Now they that died in the plague were fourteen thousand and seven hundred, beside them that died about the matter of Korah.

I Samuel 15:26—And Samuel said unto Saul, I will not return with thee; for thou hast rejected the word of the Lord, and the Lord hath rejected thee from being king over Israel.

I Samuel 15:24—And Saul said unto Samuel, I have sinned; for I have transgressed the commandment of the Lord, and thy words; because I feared the people, and obeyed their voice.

"THE RIGHT PLACE"

Jer. 3:15—And I will give you pastors according to mine heart, which shall feed you with knowledge and understanding.

Insecurity births bondage. When we use the pulpit or any platform to boost ourselves and make ourselves look better, we are abusing the position that God has given us and we do it at the expense of others. Be careful that you are not submitting yourself and your family to an overly insecure leader. It will only birth bondage in you and cause to be spiritually immobilized. And be sure you are not leading with any of the characteristics listed. Let go of your feelings and rest in what God will do for you. There is no perfect leader, but some imperfections are dangerous and should not be tolerated. Seek God's wisdom before you decide to submit to any covering. There are some things we can deal with, but there are other things that may be deadly to our purpose in God and those things must be avoided. Here are some signs of an insecure leader:

1. Improper placement of gifts and callings—Whenever people are misplaced in a ministry, it's usually on purpose. People know what God has gifted them to do, but an insecure leader usually wants to place them in areas that they are not called to so they won't do too well. This keeps people looking to the leader for direction and makes an insecure leader feel like he's still the focus of the ministry or he still has power over the people. Often times, an insecure leader will give people positions so they won't leave the church. But misplacement of gifts in a ministry keeps the people looking to a man for direction and never really looking to God.

2. Micro-managing—This is a sure sign of an insecure person. They must know what's going on at all times. They have to know what each person and ministry under them is doing and always tries to direct or lead each and every aspect of the ministry. This is to ensure that no one out shines them or no one can ever get credit for what they have done. This keeps the leader number one.

3. Plants—This is a very sad, yet very sure sign of an insecure pastor or leader. They'll put people around you to spy and tell them what you are doing. If you have a gift or calling and people are drawn to it, they will plant a person to come around you and sniff you out for them. They don't want your gift or calling to take the attention off them so they have to watch you with a "planted" person. What a shame, but oh so true.

4. Wrongfully removed—An insecure leader will move people for no reason. They will stop you if you are doing a good job or if you are too faithful to your department head because they fear that you will somehow lose your loyalty to them. They shift people around just when that person is settling into their position because they don't want you too successful in their church or ministry.

5. No fellowship—An insecure leader doesn't like fellowship with outside ministries. They find fault in everyone, but this is usually a cop out. The bottom line is, they don't want to fellowship with anyone because they fear they will lose members if their members see something better than what they are offering. So, the make every other ministry seems wrong to block any desire to fellowship with them.

6. Spiritual Abortions—An insecure leader does not birth other ministries outside of their own. Check the track record. How many pastors have come out of this ministry? How many outreach ministries have been birthed? How many have been encouraged to pursue outside missions and evangelism that will reach beyond the church doors? An insecure leader will never push anyone to go do anything outside of the church because they fear losing members to them. So, they keep

everything inside and never father outside ministries. And God forbid you try to leave this type of leader. They will make you feel like you are going to hell for leaving and there is nothing else out there.

7. Too much church—An insecure leader will always want to be at church! They love to call meetings, counsel everyone, and spend most of their family time and leisure time at the church. And they will even require you to be there at all times. When the doors open, you should be there. This is because they feel they are missing something or losing ground with the people if they don't see them. A secure leader invests in family time and allows freedom for his people to enjoy their lives and their outside interests.

8. No privacy—An insecure leader will almost always address your private issues from the pulpit. They will counsel with you and then preach your issues purposely to the people in the church. They will even call you up at times and embarrass you by dealing with your personal sins and issues before the whole church. A secure leader can handle your issues in private and not boost himself by making you look bad.

9. Masquerade—An insecure leader has to put on a mask to seem spiritual and deep. They cannot be common or seem common to the people because they strive to be feared by the membership. They depend totally on their reputation and not on the spirit of God in them. They have to make you feel less so they will feel bigger and better. It's one thing to be respected because of the Spirit of God in you, but when you demand respect, it's artificial.

10. No gifts—The number one sign of an insecure leader is, they are always worried about what people think of them. They won't even allow certain gifts to operate in the ministry because it may make others that don't flow in gifts jealous or uncomfortable. The ministry is always politically correct. And usually, there are no gifts in operations, not even in the pastor. When the pastor cannot flow in gifts, the body will not because where the head is, the body must follow.

Be careful saint's of God. What God has given you is worthy of secure leadership and you must make sure you are not wasting space in a ministry. You must make sure you are following the right person. Sure, no one is perfect, but at least we must strive for it. And beware of leaders that cannot admit mistakes! When they never mess up or never confess to error, then beware! There is not a perfect man, and a secure leader can say, "I was wrong!"

Suggested reading: **Eph. 4:11; Jer. 3:15; Jer. 12:10; Jer. 23:1.**

THE QUALIFICATION OF A DEACON

Scriptures: I Timothy 3:8,12; Acts 6:1-7; Titus 27:7-8

The meaning of the word Deacon:

The word Deacon comes from the Greek work *diakonos*. This word occurs a number of times in the Scriptures, but only four times to describe what we call deacons in the church today. Diakonos means servant, minister, waiter, or attendant. When used in an official way it describes what we call deacons of the church. In Acts, chapter six, the apostles instructed the congregation to select seven men who were to be appointed to the task of daily serving the needs of the congregation. They waited upon the people. They served the widows. They rendered active service toward solving a problem. This is the meaning of the term diakonos (deacon).

Reason for Qualifications:

The qualification for deacons that are given in I Timothy 3:8-12 and certain ideas that comes to us from Titus 2:7-8 and Acts 6, give us guidelines for the men who are responsible to care for the material aspects of God's people. Every member of the congregation should give the time and prayerful consideration necessary to carefully study God's word and their lives as potential deacons for this congregation and that they meet the qualification.

Whether a person is to be an elder, deacon, or even an evangelist in the church, a man's personal qualifications must carefully be considered. It should be remembered that these are qualifications given by God for men, not angels or men to men! None of these qualifications are out of reach for today's church members to achieve.

Elders and deacons are necessary to be appointed if they are available. If qualified men are not available they should not be appointed. No office in the church should be filled just to be filling that office. If work needs to be done, then men should be selected to do the work as in Acts chapter six.

The office of a deacon is that of a servant. Servants serve. They relieve the elders of mundane and routine affairs of the church. The men appointed in the book of Acts were appointed to do a certain task in order that the apostles would not be required to leave the Word of God to serve tables. Even though these were not specifically called deacons, we usually refer to them as they first deacons recorded in the New Testament.

The apostles brought the congregation together, set up the qualification, gave the number of men, and made the appointments. But notice carefully that it was the church, which made the selection of the men (Acts 6:3).

If we include all that is indicated in this passage, and the qualifications listed in Timothy and Titus we could list the personal qualifications for deacons as follows:

- An honest life—of good reputation (the congregation, community and neighborhood thinks well of him.)
- A spiritual person—full of wisdom (a person who is directed by that which the Spirit has revealed (Gal 5:16))
- A person with wisdom—full of wisdom (his dealings with his fellowman show a person possessing wisdom.)
- Maturity of life—the husband of one wife, good managers of their children (old enough to have children and mature enough to manage them well.)
- Gravity of conduct—must be men of dignity (honorable, venerable, of serious character)
- Simplicity and sincerity—not double-tongued (keeps the same position on all issues to all people, not telling one person one thing and another person something else.)
- Of temperate habits—not addicted to much wine (nor to be completely absorbed in any outside interest.)
- Unselfish—not fond of sordid gain (to love money is the root of all kinds of evil.)

The Office of the Deacon (Nuggets)

1. He should live a consecrated Christian life, bringing no reproach by his conduct upon the church or the cause of Christ.

2. He should attend church a minimum of 2 out of 3 services each week unless hindered by some reason, which is approved by a good conscience.
3. He should be a tither—bringing his tithe systematically to the church for the Lord's work.
4. He should be evangelistic and missionary in spirit, deeply interested in the salvation of souls at home and abroad.
5. He should be fully cooperative with the Pastor and church in a great spiritual program of advancement.
6. He should be a man who refrains from destructive criticism of his Pastor and church or its leadership, willing to settle all difficulties in a quiet and Christian manner, without hurting the cause of Christ or His church.
7. He should be able to keep in secrecy those things, which would not honor Christ, the church and the church members.
8. He should be active in the various activities of the church—Sunday school, Discipleship Training and Brotherhood.
9. He should be a man about whom people say, "He is a good Christian man."
10. He should measure up to the requirements given in I Timothy 3:8-13.

Qualifications of a Deacon
1. Be male member of this church for a minimum of one year as of January 1.
2. Be a minimum of 25 years of age as of October 1.
3. Possess the spiritual qualifications as set forth in Acts 6:3 and I Timothy 8:8-12.
4. He shall support the full program of the church, and shall be a tither.
5. He shall be the husband of one wife—having never been divorced, widowed, or never married.

Just what is a Deacon?
A Deacon is a servant, not a church boss.
The word *deacon* means *servant*. A deacon is elected not to honor a man but to honor and serve God and His church.
A Deacon is one whose character is exemplary.
Not only his life, but his reputation is a credit to the church and the Savior. His family life is a good example.

A Deacon is a spiritually minded man.
" . . . full of the Holy Spirit," the Scriptures say. The world and the deacon cannot mix without the church losing immeasurably.

A Deacon is a devoted and faithful steward of his possessions.
A deacon is "not greedy of filthy lucre." He must lead by his example if the church is to grow a membership of tithers.

A Deacon is regular in attendance at all services.
By his presence, he adds much, **by his absence he causes much harm.**

A Deacon is the Pastor's friend.
He should be counselor, confidant, comforter, companion and friend to the Pastor.

Scriptural Qualifications for Deacons

- Deacons must be serious, sincere in their talk, not addicted to strong drink or dishonest gain.
- But they must continue to hold the open secret of faith with a clear conscience.
- They, too, should first be tested till approved, and then, if they are found above reproach, they should serve as deacons.
- The wives must be serious, too, not gossips, they must be temperate and perfectly trustworthy.
- A Deacon, too, must have only one wife, and manage his children and household well.

For those who render good service win a good standing for themselves in their faith in Christ Jesus.

ACKNOWLEDGEMENTS

This, then, is not the end but the beginning of our walk of unity towards fulfilling our mission Christ has pre-destined for us. Let us use these materials to help move us into enlightenment and a mighty force for our Lord and Savior, Jesus Christ.

To my wife, Terry, without whom this work could not have been completed. I thank you with all my heart.

To my daughter, Monique Menefee, you were invaluable to me during this project. I honor the gifts you brought to help me complete this manual.

Many thanks to my pastors, Drs. Amos and Deborah Bankhead, for the instructions and guidance given to me as I regained my footing with my walk towards Christ. I love you both and honor your ministry.

Thanks to Pastors, Doctors R. Dale Kitchens and Bruce Scotten for seeing my gifts and nourishing them towards flourition. You held my hand as I steadied my walk.

AFTERWORD

As I close this manual, I leave you with this story:

After living what I felt was a decent life, my time on earth came to an end. The first thing I remember is sitting on a bench in the waiting room of what I thought to be a court house. The doors opened and I was instructed to come in and have a seat by the defense table. As I looked around, I saw the "prosecutor." He was a villainous looking gent who snarled as he stared at me. He definitely was the most evil person I have ever seen. I sat down and looked to my left and there sat my attorney, a kind and gentle looking man whose appearance seemed so familiar to me, I felt I knew him. The corner door flew open and there appeared the Judge in full flowing robes. He commanded an awesome presence as he moved across the room and I couldn't take my eyes off him. As he took his seat behind the bench, he said, "Let us begin."

The prosecutor rose and said, "My name is Satan and I am here to show you why this man belongs in hell." He proceeded to tell of lies that I told, things that I stole, and in the past when I cheated others. Satan told of other horrible perversions that were once in my life and the more he spoke, the further down in my seat I sank.

I was so embarrassed that I couldn't look at anyone, not even my own attorney, as the Devil told of sins that even I had completely forgotten about. As upset as I was at Satan for telling all these things about me, I was equally upset at my attorney who sat there silently not offering any form of defense at all. I know I had been guilty of those things, but I had done some good in my life—couldn't that at least equal out part of the harm I'd done?

Satan finished with a flurry and said, "This man belongs in hell. He is guilty of all that I have charged and there is not a person who can prove otherwise."

When it was his turn, my attorney first asked if he might approach the bench. The judge allowed this over the strong objection of Satan, and beckoned him to come forward. As he got up and started walking, I was able to see him in his full splendor and majesty. I realized why he seemed so familiar; this was Jesus representing me, my Lord and Savior.

He stopped at the bench and softly said to the judge, "Hi, Dad!" Then he turned and addressed the court. "Satan was correct in saying that this man had sinned, I won't deny any of these allegations. And yes, the wage of sin is death and this man deserves to be punished."

Jesus took a deep breath and turned to his father with outstretched arms and proclaimed, "However, I died on the cross so that this person might have eternal life and he has accepted me as his savior, so he is mine." My Lord continued with, "His name is written in the book of life and no one can snatch him from me. Satan still does not understand yet. This man is not to be given justice, but rather mercy."

As Jesus sat down, he quietly paused, looked at his father and said, "There is nothing else that needs to be done. I've done it all."

The judge lifted his mighty hand and slammed the gavel down. The following words bellowed from his lips, "This man is free. The penalty for him has already been paid in full. Case dismissed."

As my Lord led me away, I could hear Satan ranting and raving, "I won't give up! I will win the next one!"

I asked Jesus as he gave me my instructions where to go next, "Have you ever lost a case?"

Christ lovingly smiled and said, "Everyone that has come to me and asked me to represent them has received the same verdict as you. PAID IN FULL!"